Kathy,

"To Believe in God
is to build a bridge
between yourself and
everything worth being
one with."

Thank you for building a bridge
to me.

Merry Christmas

Love,
Mel
12/68

to believe in god

to believe in God

by Joseph Pintauro

Harper & Row, Publishers, New York, Evanston, & London

color by Sister Corita

FIRST EDITION

Library of Congress Catalog Card Number: 68-11741

DO NOT KILL ME
before you search my eyes
before you see through me
and I through you
for a place to be . . .

one by one our old heavens
have left us

places in hearts all we have left

We cannot live forever

outside each other
who still dream of mansions.

to believe in god

is to get high

on love enough
to look down

at your loneliness and
forget it forever.

To believe in god

is to know the world
is
round
not flat,
and there is
no edge of
anything.

up.

nowadays
to be on your way
is to be home.

egg shells are sometimes so thin
you may see out of one for a
hundred years and never know you were inside.
Some eggs are inside an egg,
and sometimes

those inside eggs have an egg
inside, which has eggs inside
of it.
Planets are egg yolks
and stars are
pin holes
in a shell.

to believe in god is to be
a lily in a sun shower
open wide
to all the horizons of the sky
at once

Catching wet
and wild the wind
and rain over the futures
from which they blew

to believe in God
is to know purple jelly beans
could hatch to yellow ostriches

and tulip bulbs break into
blooms big as moons,
or even rabbits

could produce hum... out of ha...

and

it would be all the same . . .

Easter .

to believe in

God is to get so
attached to everything
that it can't give you up.

there are some living organisms that become
born, copulate, and die all in the
space of two hours, once upon a time
one of those things
lived to the spectacular
age of three days

nine hours and
42 seconds
exactly!

to believe in god
is to know that _all_ our stars

are lucky ones.

to believe in God is

o know
the thing you are
shall make you live
and it will never
make you do anything
less.

to believe in god

is to build
a bridge between yourself
and everything worth
being
one with

to believe in god
is to have the great
that somewhere
is not stupid.

faith

Someone

to believe in God
is to have some
who knows you
and likes you
and all.

body
thru and thru
still

our minds to rest
a while, while
we mind one another's
thinking.

to believe in god
is to be one of those kids who
just refuses

to grow up and get

older and
older and
die
forever.

GREEN GREEN IS A GOD COLOR

SPRING DOESN'T COME IT'S
THE WORLD IT GOES BING
LIKE A SPRING IT GOES
BING LIKE A HIGH-PITCHED
BOING IT GOES HIGHER THAN
BING... BEING
SPLASH LIKE
A SPRING SPRING GOES
SQUIRT LIKE A LITTLE SPLASH SPRING

DOESN'T COME IT'S THE WORLD
IT SQUIRTS GREEN GREEN
IS A GOD COLOR

SUMMER IS A WHEN FOR
SPRING TO STAY ITS SPRING
WITH TIME TAKEN OUT BUT
EVEN STILL
SUMMER SWINGS LIKE A
CHILD ON A SWING SINGING WHEE IN THE BREEZE

AUTUMN IS BONG SPRING ON IT'S HEAD
ITS SPRING TUMBLING ON ITS MERRY
WAY TUMBLING
AWAY FALLING

WINTER IS NOTHING COMING
OR GOING OR STAYING
WINTER IS WINTER
THOUGH SNOW IS LIKE SPRING . . . . .

ONLY WHITE AND MAYBE COLD
WINTER IS WHEN WE MOST SHOULD
PRAY WHEN SPRING IS AWAY
AND MAY MAY IS WHAT WE GET MAY
IS A MIRACLE SO YOU SEE
SO YOU SEE SPRING
DOESN'T COME ITS THE WORLD...

day is never a time of the sun
but of the world

Sometimes there is night

night is necessary
it is nice
... in a way

God is sun like
always shining

facing up to it.

... if you look back
you can almost see the wall
of time. The moss on it

is still wet. You can smell

t.

looking forward

there are no walls so

Get on your mark, get ready

get set . . .

. . . . once, we didn't know how to believe
in a rocket ship or even a lawn mower,
make space in your brain for

tomorrow's things.

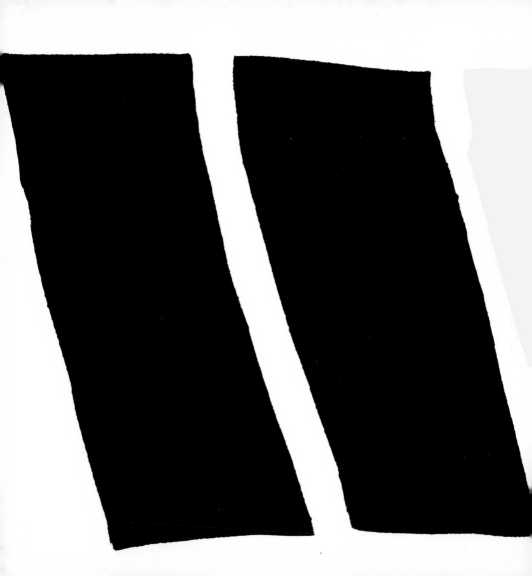

in god

is to drink

it is to eat

to believe in god
is to have a Him
to be in

which is for everyone
to have in us .

to believe in god

is to be able
to die
and not to be embarrassed.

A House you may believe in

there is a house
of glass and wood transparent
as air and built on piles
among ocean dunes
in which the floors are layed with
tiles from India and breezes of
a dozen lands pass through and
even the ocean has passed under

wicker white furniture on its deck
and huge clay pots
holding
imported
earth
and

trees

bearing

bright

Spanish

lemons

the bathroom is a place of straw
walls
and
floor
and
sun
and
geraniums

where you wash and sit in
filtered shade bare to dry

in the kitchen there are cabinets full
of clear glass dinnerware forks and
spoons of african wood,
              Chilean wine in trade
Green bottles and bread and plum
tomatoes

in the bedroom two old russian chests
and a new england vase
painted ivy full of ivy
egyptian cotton sheets on the beds
low simple beds without coverlets

three walls naked for bouncing
        sound white and
awaiting the breaker's roar
while one wall glows...

for the moon.

and you may believe
in this place although all
the lemon trees must go
to greenhouse long before the snow
when a man must find a cottage
of another kind but oh
believe until then

.... in this house

while driving from the beach once
a girl and I fell in
love with white
daisies in a field of white
daisies
and she wound up that sparkling june
day so happy
picking at the whole meadow

I lost her a second
but she reappeared a
ship with sails,
flying from both sides of her
arms so full and the wind
did so much to her hair

half way home

a sign

PICK THEM YOURSELf

caught her eye

strawberries

and I lost her again

that night my house was
jammed with strawberries and white

daisies in every vase and pot

nd as I sat there talking with friends

I noticed a flourescence.... she

leeping on the divan a child

with bare feet stained red and
red sunburned hands and hair

So flowing free and yellow
that it must have been a dim dawn

when the sun went up in London
that day.

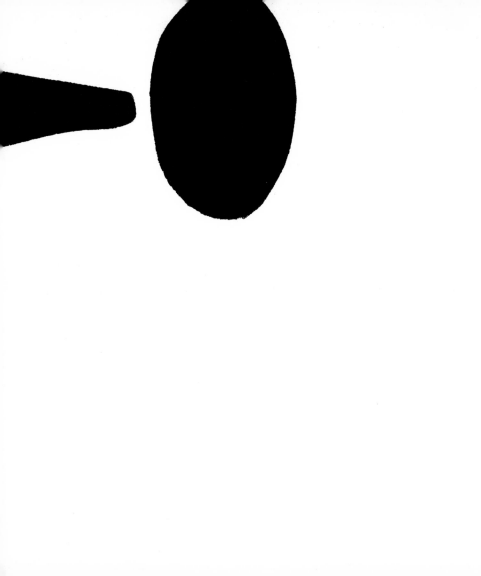

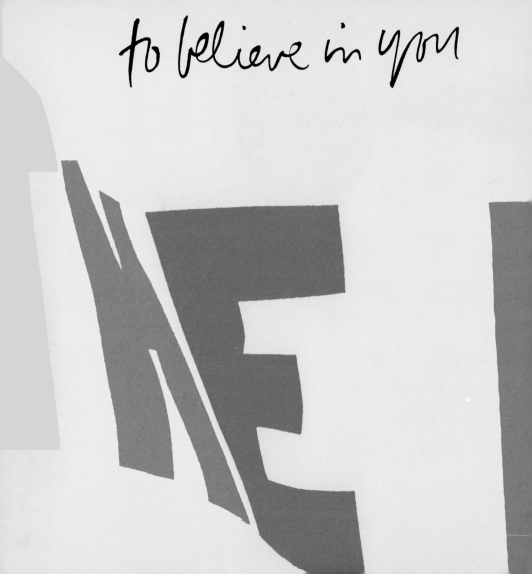

to believe in you

is more than I need
to make believing

more than making believe.